THE CENTRAL INTELLIGENCE AGENCY

THE U.S. GOVERNMENT
HOW IT WORKS

★ ★ ★

THE CENTRAL INTELLIGENCE AGENCY
THE DEPARTMENT OF HOMELAND SECURITY
THE FEDERAL BUREAU OF INVESTIGATION
THE HOUSE OF REPRESENTATIVES
THE PRESIDENCY
THE SENATE
THE SUPREME COURT

THE U.S. GOVERNMENT
HOW IT WORKS

THE CENTRAL INTELLIGENCE AGENCY

HEATHER LEHR WAGNER

CHELSEA HOUSE
PUBLISHERS
An imprint of Infobase Publishing

The Central Intelligence Agency

Chelsea House
An imprint of Infobase Publishing
132 West 31st Street
New York, NY 10001

ISBN-10: 0-7910-9282-8
ISBN-13: 978-0-7910-9282-8

Library of Congress Cataloging-in-Publication Data
Wagner, Heather Lehr.
  The Central Intelligence Agency / Heather Lehr Wagner.
     p. cm.—(The U.S. government: how it works)
  Includes bibliographical references and index.
  ISBN 0-7910-9282-8 (hardcover)
  1. United States. Central Intelligence Agency—Juvenile literature. 2. Intelligence Service—United States—Juvenile literature. I. Title. II. Series.

 JK464.16W34 2007
 327.1273—dc22

                            2006028387

Chelsea House books are available at special discounts when purchased in bulk quantities for businesses, associations, institutions, or sales promotions. Please call our Special Sales Department in New York at (212) 967-8800 or (800) 322-8755.

You can find Chelsea House on the World Wide Web at
http://www.chelseahouse.com

Series design by James Scotto-Lavino
Cover design by Ben Peterson

Printed in the United States of America

Bang NMSG 10 9 8 7 6 5 4 3 2 1

This book is printed on acid-free paper.

All links and Web addresses were checked and verified to be correct at the time of publication. Because of the dynamic nature of the Web, some addresses and links may have changed since publication and may no longer be valid.

CONTENTS

1

INTELLIGENCE IN AMERICA

In the summer of 1776, while delegates to the Continental Congress in Philadelphia debated the document that would become known as the Declaration of Independence, the commander of the Continental Army, General George Washington, was moving his force of 15,000 men south from Boston to New York. He was preparing for a major engagement in these early days of the Revolutionary War, an engagement that would pit his volunteer troops against the polished, professional, and far larger British military force commanded by General William Howe.

The Continental Army experienced a humiliating defeat, losing Long Island in a single day, suffering 300 casualties, and having 1,000 men taken prisoner. Washington's generals recommended an evacuation of Manhattan, but Washington refused, believing that a retreat at this stage would send a terrible message to the supporters of the revolution. Washington was determined to recapture all of New York.

Washington called on Lieutenant Colonel Thomas Knowlton to assemble his military unit, known as "Knowlton's Rangers." The Rangers had a reputation for being bold and fearless and were patrolling the shorelines along Manhattan at the time.

Knowlton stood before his men and explained that General Washington needed a volunteer for a dangerous mission. This volunteer would serve as a spy, slipping behind British lines and providing the Continental Army with information about troop positions and British military plans. The spy would need to provide drawings of troop movements and British fortifications, and he would need to mingle with British officers, befriending them in order to obtain vital information.

There was silence for a moment, as the men shifted uncomfortably. Then, a young schoolteacher from Connecticut stepped forward to volunteer. The man's name was Nathan Hale.

Hale was highly educated—he had graduated from Yale and served as a schoolteacher for two years. When the revolution began in Massachusetts and men from Connecticut were asked to form a militia to fight the British, Hale volunteered. He had joined the Seventh Connecticut Militia a little more than a year before and had only come to New York a few months earlier with his regiment. Soon after, he was detached for service with Knowlton's Rangers.

Many of Hale's friends tried to persuade him not to accept the assignment. Spying was considered to be one of the lowest forms of military service, not something a gentleman or a highly educated and ambitious officer would do. Hale, though, knew that the situation was desperate, and he refused to withdraw his offer.

Hale used his teaching background as the cover for his spying mission. By September 1776, he was ready to set off. He left the Continental Army and walked from Harlem Heights in New York to Norwalk, Connecticut, a journey of some 50 miles (80 kilometers) along the coast. At Norwalk, Hale found a ship that would take him across the Long Island Sound to British-occupied territory.

Hale was disguised as a traveling teacher, wearing a plain, brown suit and a round, wide-brimmed hat. He carried his diploma and his watch but left all of his other belongings behind. Hale then began his mission, slowly moving back toward New York City through British camps.

Hale was pleasant and easy-going, and he sprinkled his speech with comments designed to show those he met that he was a Loyalist—a supporter of the British military and of King George. Soon, Hale had befriended several soldiers and officers, who gradually began to tell the amiable teacher of their plans to destroy the American troops. As Hale moved through the camps, he studied the fortifications and, late at night, he made sketches of what he saw.

Finally, Hale was satisfied that he had enough information to provide General Washington with a victory over the British troops. He gathered all of his sketches and slid them into his shoes. Hale walked quickly back north until, on September 21, he reached the crossing point where he first landed a few weeks earlier, a town called The Cedars. Hale arrived early in the morning, before the boat was ready to begin ferrying passengers across the river. He slipped into a quiet Loyalist tavern for something to eat.

In the tavern was someone familiar to Hale, but he could not place the face. Hale was confident, however, that his disguise was sufficient to protect him from being recognized. Soon, Hale was eating and engaged in conversation with several other patrons. Suddenly, a waitress in the tavern looked out the window and commented that a boat had landed at the dock.

Hale was sure that this was the boat for which he was waiting. He stepped outside and was immediately surrounded by a dozen British soldiers, who ordered him to surrender. As Hale stepped onto the boat, he noticed in the crowd the man who had seemed familiar to him, a man Hale now recognized as his Loyalist cousin, Samuel Hale. Nathan Hale suddenly realized that his cousin must have betrayed him.

British soldiers prepare to hang Nathan Hale, the American patriot and spy. Hale, who had tracked and recorded British troop movements on Long Island, New York, was captured and killed by the British in September 1776. Just before his hanging, he famously said: "I only regret that I have but one life to lose for my country."

The hidden papers were soon discovered, and Hale's fate was sealed. He was returned to New York and handed over to General Howe.

Hale's calm and fearless manner impressed Howe, who offered him a full pardon if he would become a double agent and spy for the British Army. Hale refused. Howe ordered him hanged at dawn.

The next morning, Hale was taken from his jail cell to a large tree outside. A rope hung from the tree branch, and beneath the tree a grave waited for his body.

As Hale's neck was placed in the noose, his executioner asked him if he had any last words. Hale famously replied, "I only regret that I have but one life to lose for my country."

On September 22, 1776, 21-year-old Nathan Hale became the first American captured and executed for spying. A statue honoring Hale stands outside the Central Intelligence Agency today, serving as a reminder of the sacrifices that may be required of those who work in the field of intelligence.

AT HEADQUARTERS

The headquarters of one of the world's most powerful and secretive intelligence services can be found about eight miles (13 kilometers) northwest of downtown Washington, D.C. On more than 250 acres of flat, partially wooded land bordering the Potomac River in Langley, Virginia, is the Central Intelligence Agency of the United States.

The Central Intelligence Agency, or CIA as it is more commonly known, serves a critical role in the shaping of American foreign policy. The CIA is responsible for providing information related to national security issues to the U.S. president and to senior U.S. policymakers. This is done by collecting intelligence (or information) about possible foreign threats to American security.

The CIA was formally created by President Harry S. Truman when he signed the National Security Act of 1947. This act also created the office of director of central intelligence to serve as head of the U.S. intelligence community and to act as the president's principal advisor on intelligence issues related to national security.

SPIES SHAPING U.S. HISTORY

Although the creation of the CIA is relatively recent in American history, the process of gathering intelligence has played a vital role since before the United States gained its independence. General George Washington used spies, secret agents, intelligence gathering, and covert action during the Revolutionary War—Nathan Hale was one of several spies drafted by Washington.

Both Benjamin Franklin and John Jay directed secret missions and operations that provided vital information and contributed to America's success in the Revolutionary War. These early intelligence missions involved agents and double agents, acts of sabotage, and paramilitary raids against British troops and outposts. Other tools were used as well—secret codes, propaganda, and the spreading of false information.

Once the United States had achieved its independence, intelligence played an important role in ensuring that the independence lasted. George Washington, as the first American president, asked the U.S. Congress to establish a fund for clandestine (or secret) missions and activities in his first State of the Union speech. President Thomas

Jefferson used this fund in a secret plan to topple a foreign government—one of the Barbary Pirate states in North Africa—in 1804. The attempt failed.

From 1810 to 1812, James Madison used secret intelligence and paramilitary forces to try to obtain land from Spain in the territory we now know as Florida. During

NATIONAL SECURITY ACT OF 1947

★ ★ ★ ★ ★

On July 26, 1947, President Harry S. Truman signed the National Security Act, which formally ushered in a new era in defense and security policy, including the creation of the Central Intelligence Agency. The act, later amended and unclassified, includes the following points:

SEC.102A. [50 U.S.C. 403-1] There is a Central Intelligence Agency. The function of the Agency shall be to assist the Director of Central Intelligence in carrying out the responsibilities referred to in paragraphs (1) through (5) of section 103(d) of this Act.

SEC.103. (50 U.S.C. 403-3] (a) PROVISION OF INTELLIGENCE . . .

(d) HEAD OF THE CENTRAL INTELLIGENCE AGENCY. In the Director's capacity as head of the Central Intelligence Agency, the Director shall

(1) collect intelligence through human sources and by other appropriate means, except that the Agency shall have no police, subpoena, or law enforcement powers or internal security functions;

(2) provide overall direction for the collection of national intelligence through human sources by elements of the intelligence

the Civil War, both Union and Confederate forces used secret intelligence, military scouts, intercepted mail, decoded telegrams, and captured documents to gain an advantage for their side. Other information was obtained by interrogating captured prisoners and deserters. Many of the most successful spies during this period were women

community authorized to undertake such collection and, in coordination with other agencies of the Government which are authorized to undertake such collection, ensure that the most effective use is made of resources and that the risks to the United States and those involved in such collection are minimized;

(3) correlate and evaluate intelligence related to the national security and provide appropriate dissemination of such intelligence;

(4) perform such additional services as are of common concern to the elements of the intelligence community, which services the Director of Central Intelligence determines can be more efficiently accomplished centrally; and

(5) perform such other functions and duties related to intelligence affecting the national security as the President or the National Security Council may direct.

Pauline Cushman was an actress who spied for the Union forces during the Civil War. She was captured by the South but was saved three days before her scheduled execution. Cushman received an honorary major's commission from President Abraham Lincoln. During the Civil War, many of the most successful spies were women.

whose homes had been seized by troops or who were forced to serve the soldiers as cooks, nurses, or washerwomen. They were able to pass along information they had overheard from the soldiers who were occupying their homes or demanding supplies or services.

The first formal intelligence agencies that existed in the United States were directly connected to the military. Formed in the 1880s, the Office of Naval Intelligence and the Military Intelligence Division of the Army sent agents to several European cities to gather information. Sources were placed at telegraph offices like Western Union to provide information on the contents of relevant telegrams. Others worked at ports where they could observe ship movements and naval activities.

During World War I, significant funding for intelligence activities was not provided until the United States declared war on Germany in 1917. Expert intelligence, however, can take years to gather—years during which contacts need to be made, cover stories established, and people with the appropriate language and technical skills trained. Congress passed the first federal espionage law in 1917, and intelligence both during and after World War I focused on breaking codes and intercepting communications.

The Japanese bombing of Pearl Harbor in 1941 was a wake-up call to those who questioned the need for a centralized system of intelligence gathering. Pearl Harbor represented a major intelligence failure, caused by incorrect analysis of information, poor collection of intelligence,

Standing among wrecked airplanes at the Ford Island Naval Air Station at Pearl Harbor, Hawaii, sailors watched as the USS *Shaw* exploded in the background. The surprise Japanese attack on Pearl Harbor on December 7, 1941, represented a major American intelligence failure and led to the formation of what would become the Central Intelligence Agency.

confusion within the different intelligence organizations, and misinformation from Japanese sources. It was in large part because of Pearl Harbor that steps were taken to create a single agency responsible for intelligence gathering, the agency that would eventually become the CIA.

THE CIA TODAY

The modern CIA continues to focus on the vital mission of providing analysis of critical intelligence issues to America's policymakers. The CIA does this by identifying a wide range of problems or issues that might pose a threat to U.S. security or to the U.S. government. For instance, the CIA might focus on a particular terrorist organization and its activities and suspected plans. Or it might analyze biological or chemical weapons and the likelihood of certain countries to gain access to them and use them.

CIA agents translate foreign newspaper and magazine articles as well as radio and television broadcasts. They study satellite images from space to determine information like the location of planes at a foreign military base. Coded messages are intercepted and decoded. Foreigners are recruited to provide information about events or people in their native countries.

All of this intelligence is collected and studied, not only to determine current events in foreign locations but also to make informed predictions of what might happen next and how these events will impact the United States. The president and senior policymakers receive a daily report from the intelligence community, known as the President's Daily Briefing, which summarizes these key intelligence findings and concerns. The CIA does not make policy recommendations. The agency's mission is to report the intelligence. How that intelligence is used to shape policy is a decision made by the president, the State Department, and the Defense Department.

The precise budget of the CIA, as well as the number of employees who work there, is considered classified, and these numbers are not released to the public. CIA employees work not only at the headquarters in Langley, Virginia, but also in locations throughout the world. Many make no secret of their place of employment. A few, who operate undercover, conceal their roles as CIA agents from even their family and friends.

As a general in the Revolutionary War, George Washington stated that the "necessity of procuring good intelligence is apparent and need not be further urged." The CIA today remains committed to providing that "good intelligence" so vital to America's security.

2

COORDINATOR OF
INFORMATION

The beginnings of the CIA can be found in the story of America's first intelligence agency, the Office of Strategic Services (OSS). The OSS was in large part the creation of William J. "Wild Bill" Donovan. A World War I hero, Donovan was one of the first to appreciate that intelligence gathering should not be confined to wartime activity but should be a permanent part of the United States' efforts to shape a sensible foreign policy.

Donovan was born on January 1, 1883, in Buffalo, New York. He grew up in a poor Irish family and worked while attending Niagara College. He had planned to become a priest, but a mentor at Niagara College, Father William Egan, suggested that he instead consider a career in law. Donovan transferred to Columbia College and Law School at the age of 20, again working to pay for school. He earned a law degree, although his record as a football player at Columbia was far more impressive than his academic record. Future President Franklin D. Roosevelt was at Columbia at the same time as Donovan, although Roosevelt, as an older and far wealthier student, did not know Donovan well.

Donovan earned his law degree in 1907 and returned to Buffalo to practice law. Within five years, he had set up his own law firm. By 1912, Donovan and a group of his friends had asked the War Department for permission to form a cavalry troop as a division of the National Guard, although at the time Donovan had never ridden a horse. Permission was granted, and on May 7, 1912, Donovan and 41 other young men from Buffalo became Troop I, 1st Cavalry Regiment, New York National Guard. Donovan took his training so seriously that he quickly rose from Trooper Donovan to Sergeant Donovan and from Sergeant Donovan to Captain Donovan, in charge of the troop.

By 1914, Donovan's troop had been called in to assist in dealing with strikers at a railroad. It was soon clear, however, that a greater threat loomed—the possibility of war in Europe.

On July 14, 1914, the handsome and successful Donovan married Ruth Rumsey, who was from one of Buffalo's wealthiest families. World War I broke out while the couple was on their honeymoon.

MISSION TO EUROPE

In 1916, Donovan was asked to go to Europe on behalf of the John D. Rockefeller Foundation to help with war relief. Specifically, he was asked to help negotiate with politicians in London and Berlin to permit transports to pass through their territories with food and supplies for the Polish people, who were experiencing a famine because the war had interrupted their supplies. Donovan agreed to take on the task for no pay. He set sail on March 18, traveling to Southampton in England. The mission, though, ended before it had even officially begun. The British War Cabinet refused to lift the naval and economic blockade of Germany, a country through which the Rockefeller Foundation's supplies would need to travel to reach the Poles.

The U.S. ambassador to Britain, Walter Hines Page, suggested that Donovan talk to another American working for the war relief effort in London—Herbert Hoover, who would be elected president of the United States in 1928. Hoover drafted Donovan to assist in his organization's efforts to feed starving Belgians who were under German occupation. Donovan traveled to the Netherlands, which was a neutral country, and then received permission to enter occupied Belgium. He traveled in and out of the country several times, gaining an understanding of working with international organizations and learning a considerable amount about wartime conditions in Europe.

William J. "Wild Bill" Donovan commanded the "Fighting Irish" infantry regiment during World War I and received the Congressional Medal of Honor and the Distinguished Service Cross. Donovan was one of the first Americans to understand that the gathering of intelligence should not be restricted to wartime.

On June 26, 1916, Donovan was recalled to the United States. His cavalry troop had been mobilized to fight Mexican troops that had crossed into the United States. Donovan spent six months with his troop in Texas, fighting the Mexicans and also preparing for a possible deployment to Europe. Donovan was a stern leader, forcing his troops to do early-morning drills in the heat. His men marched, rode, ran, and crawled in endless practices and exercises, all the time carrying heavy gear and wearing heavy uniforms.

Donovan and his men returned to Buffalo in March 1917, but only three days later, Donovan was ordered to assume command of the 1st Battalion of the 69th "Fighting Irish" Infantry Regiment of the New York National Guard. The United States declared war on Germany in April 1917. By October, Donovan and his men were on a ship bound for England. Only a few weeks earlier, his wife had given birth to their first daughter, Patricia.

THE GREAT WAR

Donovan demonstrated extraordinary heroism and leadership throughout the time the "Fighting Irish" were stationed in Europe. His actions during World War I earned him the Congressional Medal of Honor (awarded five years after the war ended) and the Distinguished Service Cross for heroism on the battlefield in France. By the time the armistice was signed, Donovan had been promoted to colonel. He was stationed in Germany for several months after the war officially ended, finally returning to New

York in April 1919, where he marched at the head of his infantry unit as it paraded up Fifth Avenue.

Donovan went home to Buffalo and, before returning to work as a lawyer, he took his wife on a second honeymoon to Japan. Donovan had long been interested in the Far East, and the couple planned to spend time sightseeing, shopping, and relaxing. After only a few days in Tokyo, Donovan was contacted by the American ambassador. Reports of unrest in the Russian territory of Siberia concerned the U.S. government, and the ambassador needed someone with Donovan's skills and experience to help him assess the situation. Donovan quickly agreed to accompany the ambassador on his trip to Siberia.

One of the mission's central purposes was to investigate the threat to the Siberian regime from the Bolsheviks. Donovan soon realized that it did not make sense for the United States to support the corrupt and cruel Siberian government against attacks by the Bolsheviks. The Siberian people were desperate for a change, and Bolshevist propaganda had convinced them that revolution was the only way to bring them a better life. As part of his mission, Donovan reached an important conclusion—that a subversive war, a war for the hearts and minds of the people—was often more significant than a shooting war. This would form a powerful argument for an intelligence service that existed outside the parameters of a war.

A TIME OF PEACE

After his mission to Russia ended, Donovan returned to Buffalo and to his law practice. He was hired by the investment banking house J.P. Morgan to perform some intelligence work in Europe—Morgan was planning to finance some of the rebuilding of Europe and wanted information about the spread of Communism in the regions where it would be financing reconstruction efforts.

Donovan was appointed U.S. attorney for the Western District of New York, and a large part of his work involved enforcing Prohibition laws along the Canadian border. He was then appointed assistant attorney general, moving to Washington in 1925. He was especially accomplished in his handling of antitrust cases, arguing several before the Supreme Court.

In the 1928 presidential election, Donovan served as a campaign advisor for Herbert Hoover. Donovan made it clear that he was not interested in the vice presidency but that he would like to serve as attorney general. Ultimately, Hoover did not offer Donovan the post of attorney general or his second choice of a position in the administration, secretary of war. At the time there was strong anti-Catholic prejudice in many parts of the United States, and Hoover came under intense pressure not to appoint a Catholic to a senior post in his administration. Deeply disappointed, Donovan returned to Buffalo and to his law career.

By the late 1930s, Donovan had made several trips to a Europe once more threatened by war. In 1940, his

William J. Donovan believed that the United States should have
a single agency charged with gathering and interpreting intelligence—an idea that met with resistance from the military intelligence
agencies and the Federal Bureau of Investigation. In June 1941,
President Franklin D. Roosevelt created the Office of the Coordinator of Information, an agency similar to what Donovan envisioned, and
Roosevelt named Donovan as its director.

daughter Patricia died after a car accident. Only a few months later, France surrendered to invading German forces, and the Battle of Britain began.

COORDINATOR OF INFORMATION

Donovan had long maintained contact with senior officials in the British government. He was not closely connected to the president, Franklin D. Roosevelt, but British officials believed that, if anyone could influence American officials to enter the war on the side of Great Britain, Donovan was the man. He was invited to travel to Great Britain and soon was given access to the British intelligence operations. He traveled several times to British territories around the world and then met with Roosevelt to share what he had observed.

At the time, intelligence gathering was considered a wartime activity in the United States, and so it was the responsibility of the armed forces. Each of the individual branches of the U.S. military had its own intelligence service. There was no single agency charged with gathering and interpreting information, as existed in Great Britain. Donovan believed that this type of secret agency was vital to American interests and that he was the man to lead it.

As soon as news of these plans spread, an attempt was made to bring them to a quick end by the Office of Naval Intelligence, the Army's intelligence chief, and by the head of the Federal Bureau of Investigation (FBI), J. Edgar Hoover, who was in the process of setting up his own FBI intelligence offices outside the United States.

ROOSEVELT AND DONOVAN

President Franklin D. Roosevelt and William Donovan shared similar ideas about the value of intelligence in wartime and peacetime. A week before Roosevelt's death in April 1945, he wrote a memo to Donovan authorizing him to continue planning for an intelligence service that would exist after World War II:

> Apropos of your memorandum of November 18, 1944, relative to the establishment of a central intelligence service, I should appreciate your calling together the chiefs of the foreign intelligence and internal security units in the various executive agencies, so that a consensus of opinion can be secured.
>
> It appears to me that all of the ten executive departments, as well as the Foreign Economic Administration, and the Federal Communications Commission have a direct interest in the proposed venture. They should all be asked to contribute their suggestions to the proposed centralized intelligence service.
>
> President Franklin D. Roosevelt
> Memorandum to Maj. Gen. William J. Donovan
> 5 April 1945

But it was clear that Donovan, who had spent extensive time in the war zone, knew far more about what was going on there than any representatives from these competing intelligence offices. Donovan's proposal was that whoever was in charge of the intelligence service must be appointed by the president and directly responsible to the president alone. The agency that Donovan envisioned would have its own source of funding—funding specific to foreign investigations. The way these funds would be spent should be secret, subject only to presidential approval.

Donovan was clear that this agency was not to take over domestic work done by the FBI or the kind of intelligence gathering done by Army and Navy intelligence. It should, however, provide a focal point for intelligence, coordinating and interpreting it.

On June 18, 1941, President Roosevelt created a new branch of government, to be known as the Office of Coordinator of Information (COI). William Donovan was to be its director. He was to receive no salary for his work, but instead would receive reimbursement for any expenses necessary to his work. The new agency was charged with collecting and analyzing all information and data that had a bearing upon national security. It was also charged with making this information and data available to the president and to other officials and departments upon the president's instruction. The COI was also authorized to carry out any additional activities necessary to obtain information vital to national security.

3

THE OSS

William J. Donovan was clear about exactly what kind of people he wanted to hire for the new intelligence agency. The people he hired were men and women (though principally men) he knew and trusted—wealthy, educated at the finest American colleges and universities, and usually Republican. They were lawyers, bankers, and professors, as well as elite representatives from many diverse fields. One of the first recruits was Pulitzer Prize-winning playwright Robert E. Sherwood, who served as the head of the radio propaganda department. Other recruits included James Roosevelt, a son of President Franklin D. Roosevelt; Estelle Frankfurter, sister of a Supreme Court justice; and two Hollywood directors—John Ford (director of *The Grapes of Wrath*) and Merian C. Cooper (director of *King Kong*).

Pulitzer Prize-winning playwright Robert E. Sherwood, seen in this 1936 photograph, was recruited by William Donovan to serve as head of the radio propaganda department in the Office of the Co-ordinator of Information. Donovan hired a diverse group of talented, educated, and successful people to work in his agency.

Donovan was skilled at finding and hiring a diverse group of highly talented, very successful individuals who, in nearly every case, agreed to work for the government at a far lower salary than they would have received in their respective fields. When the Office of the Coordinator of Information was first created, it was thought that the intelligence agency would have about 90 employees; by December 15, 1941, the staff actually numbered 596, according to Anthony Cave Brown's book, *The Last Hero: Wild Bill Donovan*.

Although these first staff members were highly skilled, given their backgrounds, they were not necessarily highly skilled in the areas we traditionally think of as intelligence work. Most had never worked for the government; some had never been out of the country. They knew little about creating and maintaining a "cover," or false identity, how to work with codes, or how to handle a silenced pistol.

The importance of a centralized intelligence agency became clear when the United States was attacked in December 1941 at Pearl Harbor. The various military intelligence agencies had pieces of information that, had they been strung together by an experienced and dedicated staff, should have provided warning of the attack.

Despite this, there were continual internal political struggles over who precisely would be given access to top-secret information and when. On June 13, 1942, President Roosevelt decided to make his wishes clear. The COI was no more. In its place, he created the Office of Strategic Services, now to be controlled not by the White House but by the Joint Chiefs of Staff, the highest-ranking members of each branch of the armed services. Donovan was no longer to oversee propaganda; instead the OSS had two missions: to collect and analyze strategic intelligence for the Joint Chiefs, and to plan and direct special operations required by the Joint Chiefs.

WORLD AT WAR

With the attack on Pearl Harbor, the United States entered World War II. Early OSS missions focused on French territory in North Africa—in an effort to occupy the territory with Allied forces without inspiring Germany to move in and try to occupy the region.

Another mission involved Allen Dulles, a key OSS agent who would later become a director of the CIA. Dulles was charged with traveling to Bern, the capital of neutral Switzerland, and making contacts to gather information about what was happening in Germany and in the main cities of Germany's allies, Japan and Italy.

During this period, intelligence operations began to focus on computer work, as well as human work. Computers known by names like Ultra and Colossus were revolutionizing intelligence work. The computers helped to break codes and, through the use of databases, aided in checking and determining the accuracy of the secret information the OSS was gathering. Computers did not replace agents like Dulles; a critical role remained for humans in making contacts, enlisting others to join the spy network, and other tasks.

During a 1996 visit, the Duke of Kent *(right)* was shown the output writer of the 15-foot-long, World War II-era, code-breaking computer known as the Colossus. During the war, the use of computers first became important in intelligence work, though the need for human agents remained essential.

By 1943, the OSS had operations spread throughout the regions affected by the war. The agency was divided into five branches with five focuses: Secret Intelligence (which gathered the information); Research and Analysis (which prepared reports and estimates about the war); Counter-espionage (which protected the OSS from enemy secret agents); Special Operations (which conducted sabotage and subversion); and Morale Operations (which helped spread information that would attack the enemy's will to fight and its belief in the war).

The OSS experienced multiple successes, but criticism was still aimed at Donovan and the agency he headed. This criticism would not be isolated; much of it is still reflected in modern debates about the CIA. There was criticism of the agency because civilian employees were handling work so vital to the military's efforts. There was criticism of Donovan's politics and his willingness to form contacts with Communists and members of other "undesirable" groups to obtain information. There was criticism of the OSS's large budget and the lack of information on how and where the money was being spent. There was criticism of the strong ties that Donovan had built between the OSS and the British secret service. And the question was raised of whether the United States should have a single, central intelligence agency or several small, specialized agencies that focused on different aspects of intelligence gathering.

Some of the OSS's successes involved spreading false information about Allied war plans. The OSS was able to convince German powers that the Allies were planning an attack through the Balkans in Eastern Europe. In fact, the Allies were planning to invade Europe from northeastern and southern France. German forces were positioned along the Balkan front in preparation for the rumored attack. Other OSS efforts included a plan to create an anti-Nazi revolution in Hungary, a country that was a key ally of Adolf Hitler's. The OSS helped gather intelligence about the German Army and about the German efforts to exterminate European Jews.

By the spring of 1945, OSS agents were scattered throughout the world, and the OSS units, in the three years since their creation, had developed strong expertise in areas like secret communications, secret finances, supply chains, counterespionage, and sabotage. Donovan was already looking ahead to what would come after the war, and he began to consider the key points that argued for the creation of a permanent American intelligence agency, one that would exist after the war ended. Donovan believed that the United States needed to know what was going on in foreign nations; that a single agency should be responsible for gathering and interpreting this intelligence; that the director of this agency should be appointed by the president; that representatives from the State, War (later Defense), and Navy departments should help guide it; that it should be responsible for secret intelligence, counterespionage, code-breaking, and subversive operations; that it should have its own independent system of communications and access to both specific and nonspecific funding; that it should not perform clandestine work within the United States; that it should not have a police function; and that this agency should be the OSS. Ultimately, these points (except the last one) would be honored in the creation of the CIA.

Unfortunately, Donovan's proposal was leaked to the media. Major newspapers soon carried headlines of plans for a "super spy system" and warnings that "Sleuths Would Snoop on U.S. and the World" and "Super Gestapo

Agency Is Under Consideration," according to *The Last Hero: Wild Bill Donovan*. Donovan was furious, but the damage was done and any talk of creating a permanent intelligence agency was postponed until public furor had calmed down.

On April 12, 1945, President Roosevelt died suddenly. Donovan had lost his biggest supporter, the man who would probably have created an intelligence agency under the terms Donovan had suggested and with Donovan as its director. Roosevelt's successor, Harry Truman, did not have the same relationship with Donovan. Shortly after the war ended, Truman made it clear that he had his own plans for a post-war intelligence agency and his own idea of the best man to run it.

On September 20, 1945, Truman signed an executive order eliminating the OSS.

THE CREATION OF THE CIA

Although Truman eliminated the OSS, saying he had his own ideas for a "peacetime" intelligence agency, the agency that was ultimately created from the ashes of the OSS—the CIA—owed much to its predecessor and the man who led it. The CIA would closely resemble the kind of agency Donovan had outlined—an independent government agency headed by a civilian, serving the president, with highly trained personnel skilled in economic, political, and military intelligence, whose work was focused outside American borders.

THE RIGHT TO KNOW

While William Donovan and President Harry Truman disagreed on what shape the peacetime intelligence agency would take and who its director would be, Truman fully understood the value of intelligence gathering—and the need to preserve the secrecy of classified intelligence—as he stressed in this October 1951 news conference:

"Whether it be treason or not, it does the United States just as much harm for military secrets to be made known to potential enemies through open publication, as it does for military secrets to be given to an enemy through the clandestine operations of spies....

"I do not believe that the best solution can be reached by adopting an approach based on the theory that everyone has a right to know our military secrets and related information affecting the national security."

Rear Admiral Roscoe H. Hillenkoetter was Truman's choice for the first director of the CIA. Several intelligence failures haunted this new agency—the Berlin crisis of 1948 that led to the division of the city between Western influence and Soviet influence; the failure to predict the Soviet Union's development of the atomic bomb; the inadequate preparation for the Korean War, and the subsequent lack of preparation for China's entry into that war; the lack of information about Russian development of a strategic air force and its detonation of a hydrogen bomb; and the

Allen Dulles, who was a key agent in the Office of Strategic Services under William Donovan, became the director of the Central
Intelligence Agency in 1953. He was one of many former Donovan
protégés who would go on to play prominent roles in the CIA.

lack of information about the situation in Indochina (the region that would later be known as Vietnam and would draw the United States into a major conflict).

Donovan returned to his private law practice after the war ended, but he never completely abandoned his hope of becoming director of central intelligence. His hopes would be disappointed, but he continued to respond when his country called, agreeing to serve as ambassador to Thailand in 1953 and providing valuable information about conditions in Southeast Asia. When his health began to fail, he resigned and returned to the United States in August 1954.

By 1957, Donovan's mental and physical health had deteriorated. In honor of his service, President Dwight Eisenhower awarded Donovan the National Security Medal, making him the only man in U.S. history to win the top four medals for courage and public service—the National Security Medal, the Congressional Medal of Honor, the Distinguished Service Cross, and the Distinguished Service Medal. He died on February 8, 1959, and is buried at Arlington National Cemetery.

Although he never served as the head of the CIA, Donovan today is known as "the Father of American Intelligence" for his role in the creation of the CIA's predecessor, the OSS. A full-length oil portrait of Donovan hangs in the CIA alongside pictures of the men who have served as the agency's directors. Many of the men who served under Donovan in the OSS would go on to head the CIA, including Allen Dulles, who served as the director of central intelligence under Presidents Dwight Eisenhower and John F. Kennedy; Richard Helms, who worked as a case officer in the OSS and became director of central intelligence under Presidents Lyndon Johnson and Richard Nixon; William Colby, who worked for the OSS in France and Norway during World War II and directed the CIA for Nixon and President Gerald Ford; and William Casey, who had served as Donovan's chief of secret intelligence in London and later was director of central intelligence for President Ronald Reagan.

4

THE HISTORY
OF THE CIA

On July 26, 1947, President Harry Truman signed into law an act that would dramatically change the ways in which future presidents would analyze and respond to international politics. This act—the National Security Act of 1947—combined the Department of the Navy and the Department of War into a single National Military Establishment (which would eventually be renamed the Department of Defense), headed by the newly created position of secretary of defense. A new branch of the military was also established—the Air Force.

The act also created the National Security Council, designed to advise and assist the president on foreign policy and provide a forum for coordination of national security issues. Finally, the act also created a peacetime intelligence agency to be known as the Central Intelligence Agency (CIA).

After the OSS was disbanded, Truman formed the Central Intelligence Group (CIG) in January 1946. Its focus was to conduct clandestine activities, principally to provide an advance warning of threats to the United States. It was led by Rear Admiral Sidney W. Souers, who had served as deputy chief of naval intelligence. The CIG was overseen by representatives of the president, the secretary of war, the secretary of the navy, and the secretary of state. The CIG, however, failed to function effectively. Each of the separate departments charged with overseeing the CIG had its own intelligence service, and the FBI had set up its own intelligence-gathering offices in Latin America. With so many competing departments trying to preserve their own intelligence divisions, the CIG lacked the power or access to function appropriately.

Through the passage of the 1947 National Security Act, the newly created CIA was given independence and direct reporting status to the president—which the CIG had lacked. The act made the CIA responsible for coordinating all U.S. intelligence activities, and for collecting, analyzing, and distributing that intelligence as necessary. The act named the director of central intelligence as the head of the intelligence community, head of the CIA, and the principal presidential advisor on intelligence matters. The first director of central intelligence was Rear Admiral Roscoe H. Hillenkoetter, who had served in naval intelligence in the Pacific during World War II.

Two years later, an additional act—the Central Intelligence Agency Act of 1949—was passed to clarify the terms of the budget available to the CIA. Under this act, the CIA was granted the ability to use confidential accounting and administrative procedures and was not required to follow the same procedures that dictated how most government agencies spent federal funds. This act ensured that how and when the CIA spent its funds would remain confidential.

In 1953, an additional amendment was made to the National Security Act. This involved the appointment of a deputy director of central intelligence. The deputy director was to perform whatever tasks the director assigned and to fill in when the director was absent because of vacation or disability, or because the position of director was vacant. The deputy director was to be appointed by the president, subject to Senate consent.

More recently, the Intelligence Reform and Terrorism Prevention Act of 2004 created two separate positions—director of national intelligence and director of the Central Intelligence Agency. The director of the Central Intelligence Agency now reports to the director of national intelligence.

COLD WAR

Truman's concern about ensuring the coordination of intelligence gathering was inspired in large part by the Cold War. After World War II ended, the Soviet Union and

Residents of West Berlin *(at right)* watched in August 1961 as East German construction workers built a section of the Berlin Wall. The wall stood for 28 years as a symbol of the separation between the Communist sphere of influence and the capitalist West.

the United States emerged as the two dominant "super-powers" in the world. Many nations in Eastern Europe that had been occupied by Nazi troops during the war fell under Soviet influence, triggering fears in the United States that the Soviet political philosophy—Communism—would become a global force.

This period—from 1947 to about 1991, when the Soviet Union began to break apart—is known as the Cold War because direct armed conflict never took place between

COLD WAR INTELLIGENCE

★ ★ ★ ★ ★

After World War II, U.S. intelligence efforts focused on the Soviet Union and actions that were perceived as expansionist or aggressive. There was fear and uncertainty about whether this Cold War might lead to armed conflict. This memo from Rear Admiral Roscoe Hillenkoetter, director of central intelligence, to President Harry Truman, declassified in 1978, reflects the focus of intelligence analysts on Soviet activities:

TOP SECRET
16 March 1948
MEMORANDUM FOR THE PRESIDENT
The Central Intelligence Agency and the intelligence organizations of the Departments of State, War, Navy and Air Force have reassessed Soviet intentions for the next sixty days and concur in the following conclusions with respect to the possibility of Soviet military action:

the two world powers. Instead, they competed through a race to acquire and develop conventional and nuclear weapons. They formed alliances with other nations. They used trade embargoes and economic incentives. Although the two nations did not engage in direct combat, they did fight indirectly in various conflicts and wars, often offering financial assistance and supplies to competing sides in civil wars (including the Korean War, the Vietnam War, the war between the Soviets and Afghans in Afghanistan,

a   An examination of all pertinent available information has produced no reliable evidence that the USSR intends to resort to military action within the next sixty days.

b   The weight of logic, as well as evidence, also leads to the conclusion that the USSR will not resort to military action within the next sixty days.

c   There is, nevertheless, the ever present possibility that some miscalculation or incident may result in military movements toward areas at present occupied by the USSR.

R.H. Hillenkoetter
Rear Admiral, US
Director of Central Intelligence

and conflicts in Nicaragua and El Salvador). Espionage and propaganda also played important roles in the Cold War. The Berlin Wall that once divided the city between West Germany and East Germany was a clear example of the division that separated Communism from capitalism.

As the Cold War began, much of the CIA's efforts focused on gathering intelligence about the Soviet Union—information about the Soviet military status; the location of roads, railroads, bridges, factories and airports; and the backgrounds of key political figures. In the years immediately after World War II, many of the key CIA sources were prisoners of war and refugees. Gradually, though, the CIA needed to replace these often-unreliable sources of information.

The CIA soon began to recruit defectors and Soviet citizens living in the West. These agents were given fictional lives and backgrounds and the proper documents to support their stories if questioned by Soviet officials or the police. They were trained in the particular skills they would need to provide vital information—identifying different types of planes; sending and receiving secret messages; taking photographs with hidden cameras. These secret agents were then dropped into Soviet territory and set to work.

Knowing that the Soviets would try a similar strategy, the CIA also focused on counterespionage work. At a time when concern about the Communist influence in the United States was approaching paranoia, the CIA concentrated on preserving its own security to ensure that

Communist agents were unable to penetrate it or recruit its employees to provide information.

The CIA also worked hard to recruit spies in the countries allied with the Soviet Union, obtaining sources of information in Eastern Europe, China, and North Korea. The goal was for the CIA to have informants in Communist party offices, economic ministries, police and military offices, and railway and postal offices.

These efforts were not always successful. The Soviets were aware of the CIA's aim to penetrate their organizations and similarly placed their own informants in refugee groups. When someone had been identified as a spy, false information might be given to him or her.

ORGANIZING THE AGENCY

Because of the confidential and covert nature of its work, CIA successes were seldom known and publicized. It was the failures—the moments when the United States was seemingly unprepared for world events—that were exposed. One of the most critical was the CIA's failure to clearly predict the outbreak of the Korean War in 1950.

In response to this failure, General Walter Bedell Smith, the second director of central intelligence, undertook a critical reorganization of the agency to correct what had been a too-tentative approach to intelligence analysis. CIA agents had felt pressure to reach an agreement on an issue in order to present the president or senior policymakers with a single, unified recommendation or prediction. This

U.S. Marines crossed the Han River in a full-scale drive toward Seoul, the then-Communist-held capital of South Korea. An early failure of the new CIA was that it did not clearly predict the outbreak of the Korean War in 1950. As a result, the CIA director, Walter Bedell Smith, reorganized the agency's approach to intelligence analysis.

meant that research and analysis that did not support the final conclusion was often brushed aside, resulting in a final product that failed to present multiple possible situations or predictions. Smith reorganized the CIA's analytical and estimation procedures, ordering the staff to stop producing huge research papers stuffed with known facts and instead provide brief and relevant papers.

With the outbreak of the Korean War, CIA agents were soon operating in Korea, China, and surrounding areas. The information they provided was valuable to the military campaign and helped strengthen what had previously been a competitive relationship between the military and the CIA.

During the 1950s, the CIA's focus expanded to a more global effort to halt the spread of Communism. It had once concentrated on predicting threats to U.S. security and dealing with crises when they arose; now its mission included a broader effort to stop Communism not only in Europe and in nations bordering the Soviet Union and China but also throughout the world. Efforts focused on combating Communist infiltration of the Philippines, Latin America, foreign labor unions, and foreign student movements.

Under President Eisenhower, CIA Director Allen Dulles favored an emphasis on covert operations. He developed the CIA's counterintelligence branch (which works to identify foreign spies and prevent them from passing information while protecting the United States' own intelligence operations).

By the 1960s, the CIA began to focus on using developments in technology to aid in the intelligence-gathering process. Although political intelligence remained vital, a similar need existed for facts and data that technology could be used to obtain. Resources and talent were dedicated to taking advantage of developments in electronics, flight engineering, space research, and computer science.

COVERT OPERATIONS

Covert operations also formed an important part of CIA efforts during the 1960s. One such operation involved the attempts to overthrow the government of Fidel Castro in Cuba. The presence of Castro, a dictator with ties to the Soviet Union, so close to U.S. soil alarmed senior policy-makers, and a decision was made to remove Castro from leadership through a series of ultimately unsuccessful operations. These included attempts to assassinate Castro and an attempt to land anti-Castro Cuban troops at the Bay of Pigs in Cuba. The CIA played instrumental roles in both, and the failure of these operations proved politically damaging to the CIA.

As American involvement in the war in Vietnam increased under President Lyndon Johnson, so too did CIA operations in Vietnam. A posting in Vietnam became important to career advancement—ambitious CIA personnel all wanted to spend time working in Vietnam. Much of the focus was on running counterinsurgency programs, collecting intelligence on Communist North Vietnam, and training the South Vietnamese in paramilitary techniques.

President Richard Nixon distrusted the CIA and preferred to consolidate intelligence control with the National Security Council (NSC) and its director, Henry Kissinger. Although this move reflected Nixon's personal preferences, the NSC and the CIA would often clash over control of intelligence under future presidents, and the role of serving as the president's key advisor on intelligence matters

Because of the clandestine nature of its work, the achievements of the CIA are not often publicized; only the agency's failures gain notice. Here, Cuban leader Fidel Castro jumps from a tank near the Bay of Pigs in April 1961. The botched Bay of Pigs invasion, which sought to remove Castro from power, hurt the CIA politically.

was no longer firmly the responsibility of the director of the CIA.

By the 1970s, the essence of the CIA had also changed. No longer an agency dependent on human intelligence sources—on spies and informants—the CIA was conduct-ing much of its work by satellite and electronic intelligence monitoring. A quick, dramatic intervention in a crisis or a region was no longer the focus; instead, intelligence was gathered as part of a long-term process that might take months or years.

A key component of the CIA's success was its ability to remain independent. The CIA director served the presi-dent, but in general CIA directors did not come and go with each new presidential administration. Public perception of the CIA, however, changed during Nixon's presidency.

On June 17, 1972, the Democratic National Committee headquarters in the Watergate building in Washington was burglarized, and evidence soon proved that White House staff members and perhaps Nixon himself might have connections to the men who staged the break-in. Nixon tried to have the CIA stop the Department of Jus-tice investigation, claiming that it was a matter of national security. It was also discovered that several of the men who had broken into the Watergate headquarters had ties to the CIA; two of the men were former CIA employees.

The Watergate scandal ultimately led to Nixon's resig-nation and a very different public perception of the CIA. Suddenly, questions were being raised about exactly what kind of work the CIA was doing, whether the agency was authorized to assassinate people, and whether and why CIA agents were operating in the United States. A conflict arose—a conflict that still sparks debate today: in an open society like America, what role (if any) should be played by an agency charged with espionage?

With new public scrutiny and pressure, the CIA gradually shifted to a more cautious approach to its mission. The focus changed to technical collection of intelligence, while covert operations and clandestine activities quietly faded into the background. Concern was high about self-protection, and missions often were measured by whether they were clearly legal and whether they had received full congressional approval.

Under President Jimmy Carter, most of the staff members responsible for clandestine operations were fired. Carter did not want the CIA to engage in covert action; instead he believed that should a crisis arise elsewhere in the world, the United States should respond with diplomatic and, if necessary, military intervention, not secret CIA actions. The weakened CIA was unable to accurately assess the situation in Iran in 1979 that led to revolution, the establishment of an anti-American Islamic government, and the capture of American hostages.

MODERN HISTORY

The CIA at the end of the twentieth century remained an agency that relied heavily on technology, placing less of an emphasis on human sources of intelligence. Analysis focused on Soviet expansion in Afghanistan and Central

CIA counter-intelligence officer Aldrich Ames is seen in an FBI video walking through a shopping mall to meet a Soviet contact. Ames passed secrets to the Soviets for nearly 10 years; his betrayal cost at least 10 U.S. agents their lives.

America, and then, with the collapse of the Soviet Union, on the rise of international terrorist organizations.

In 1994, CIA employee Aldrich Ames was unmasked as a Soviet spy. Ames had served as head of the Soviet branch of the counterintelligence group at CIA headquarters and was responsible for directing the analysis of Soviet intelligence operations. Ames had access to top-secret information about CIA counterintelligence inside and outside the Soviet Union. The information he passed to the Soviets would cost at least 10 agents their lives and damage CIA operations for nearly 10 years. Ames was convicted of spying and was sentenced to life imprisonment.

Following the September 11, 2001, terrorist attacks on the United States, the CIA and the FBI came under heavy criticism for their failure to anticipate the attacks. President George W. Bush formed a joint congressional intelligence committee to investigate the events that led up to the attacks. As a result, a separate position was created—the director of national intelligence—to coordinate all intelligence activities carried out by the various governmental agencies. The director of the Central Intelligence Agency now reports to the director of national intelligence.

5

INSIDE
THE CIA

Through several decades of shifting political demands and international crises, the Central Intelligence Agency has provided successive presidents with information on global events. The headquarters of the CIA is in Langley, Virginia, on more than 250 acres of land eight miles outside of Washington, D.C.

Despite its proximity to Washington, the area surrounding the CIA headquarters is secluded and heavily guarded. The original headquarters was completed in 1963 and contained more than a million square feet of space. Because additional work space and more parking areas were needed, two six-story office towers were built

The headquarters of the CIA is formally known as the George Bush Center for Intelligence, named after President George H.W. Bush, who served as director of central intelligence. The headquarters is on 250 acres of land eight miles northwest of Washington, D.C.

into a hillside behind the original headquarters building. This expansion was completed in 1991.

In 1999, the CIA headquarters was formally named the George Bush Center for Intelligence. This honor acknowledges the contributions to the CIA of President George H.W. Bush, who served as director of central intelligence from January 1976 to January 1977.

The main entrance to the CIA is through the lobby of the Original Headquarters Building. On the floor of the lobby is a large granite seal of the CIA. The seal measures 16 feet (5 meters) in diameter. It has been the official symbol of the CIA since February 17, 1950. Within the seal are three important symbols: the eagle, which stands for strength and alertness; the shield, a symbol for defense; and the 16-point compass star, representing how intelligence from around the world comes together at a central point.

An underground tunnel connects the Original Head-quarters Building with the Headquarters Auditorium. The auditorium has a distinctive dome shape; CIA employees sometimes call it "the bubble." This auditorium is where awards ceremonies, conferences, and speeches to CIA staff are given; it can seat up to 470 people.

REMEMBERING THOSE WHO HAVE SERVED

Several memorials are on the grounds of the CIA to honor staff members who have given their lives while working for the agency. On the west side of the main CIA entrance is the Route 123 Memorial, dedicated to two CIA officers—Frank Darling and Lansing Bennett—who were shot and killed by a terrorist while waiting to enter the main gate to the CIA on January 25, 1993.

On a hillside between the Original Headquarters Building and the auditorium is the Memorial Garden, a lovely space that combines natural and landscaped plants and a large fishpond. This garden is intended as a memorial for all intel-ligence officers and contractors who served their country.

Inside the entrance of the Original Headquarters Build-ing, to the right, is the CIA Memorial Wall, a simple wall

On the floor of the lobby to the Original Headquarters Building is the seal of the CIA. The eagle represents strength and alertness while the shield represents defense. The 16-point star shows how intelligence from around the world comes together at a central point.

sculpture framed by the American flag on the left and the flag of the CIA on the right. The wall contains the message: "In Honor of Those Members of the Central Intelligence Agency Who Gave Their Lives in the Service of Their Country." Below the words are 83 stars, one for each CIA officer who died while in service. Underneath the stars is a glass case containing the Book of Honor, which lists the names of the 48 officers whose identities can be revealed. Even after their deaths, the identities of the remaining 35 officers must continue to be kept secret

WHEN A NEW STAR IS ADDED

The CIA Memorial Wall recognizes those CIA officers who gave their lives in service to the country with a star. When a new officer is to be honored, a stone carver uses chisels, drills, paints, and polishers to add a star to the wall.

First, the carver uses a template to trace the new star on the wall. All of the stars are precisely the same size—2¼ inches tall, 2¼ inches wide, and a half-inch deep. Each star is separated from the others by six inches, and all the rows of stars are also six inches apart.

The carver uses a pneumatic air hammer and a chisel to carve out the traced star. When this is completed, the carver cleans the dust from the star and then sprays the star with a shadow-gray paint to match the tint of the stone on the wall.

A memorial ceremony is held each year at the CIA. As part of this ceremony, any new stars that have been added in the previous year have their official unveiling.

to avoid compromising ongoing investigations or revealing the identity of other secret agents.

Directly across the lobby from the CIA Memorial Wall is the Office of Strategic Services Memorial. This memorial consists of a single star and a glass-encased book listing the names of the 116 men and women who gave their lives during World War II while working for the OSS. The book is held open by a black ribbon to which is attached the OSS uniform patch. To the right of the memorial is a statue of William Donovan, the head of the OSS.

HONORING THE LEADERS

Throughout the CIA are numerous portraits, statues, and plaques that honor some of the notable men who have led the agency. On the north wall of the main lobby is a bas-relief honoring Allen Dulles, the fifth and longest-serving

President George W. Bush *(right)* and Porter Goss, then the director of the CIA, visited the CIA Memorial Wall in March 2005. The wall currently has 83 stars, one for each CIA officer who died in the line of service. In the glass case is the Book of Honor, which lists the names of those officers whose identities can be revealed.

director of central intelligence. Dulles served as director from February 1953 to November 1961; it was his vision of a college-like campus for intelligence work that resulted in the creation of the original CIA Headquarters at Langley.

George H.W. Bush holds a unique position of having served as a director of central intelligence and then as president. A bust of President George H.W. Bush stands at the top of the steps of the main lobby of the Original Headquarters Building.

Former Director of Central Intelligence William J. Casey is honored with a plaque on the north wall of the New Headquarters Building lobby. The plaque shows Casey and is sculpted from green serpentine stone. The plaque's location in the New Headquarters Building acknowledges Casey's role in overseeing the design and construction of this expansion to the CIA's facilities.

In one of the corridors that connect the old and new headquarters buildings is the DCI Portrait Gallery. The gallery contains portraits of all of the men who have served as directors of central intelligence (DCI). Each director personally selects the artist who will paint his portrait; the portraits are painted only after the director has completed his time in office. The gallery also includes a portrait of William Donovan, head of the OSS.

INTELLIGENCE ARTIFACTS

The CIA Headquarters contains many fascinating artifacts from decades of intelligence work. There is a Cold War Exhibit near the main lobby of the Original Headquarters

Building that displays a wide range of clandestine espionage artifacts from the United States, the former Soviet Union, and East Germany. There is a Berlin Wall Monument near the southwest entrance to the Original Headquarters Building, along a path that many employees use each day to enter and exit the CIA. This monument is designed to mimic the original Berlin Wall; the west side of the wall is covered with bright graffiti, while the east side is plain and stark. The three sections of concrete that make up the monument were removed from the original Berlin Wall in November 1989.

There is a CIA Museum (open only to employees) in the New Headquarters Building that contains artifacts from the OSS and the CIA. Among the items are artifacts that reflect the career of William Donovan, items used by the OSS, and artifacts from the end of the Cold War and the Persian Gulf War.

In the northwest corner of the New Headquarters Building is *Kryptos*, a sculpture by artist James Sanborn that is dedicated to the theme of intelligence gathering. The bulk of the sculpture is a large, S-shaped copper screen that looks like a piece of paper coming out of a printer. Several enigmatic messages, written in different codes, are inscribed on this piece of "paper." Over the years, CIA employees have gotten enjoyment out of trying to "break the code" contained in the sculpture.

Finally, personnel at the CIA can take advantage of its extensive research library, which contains about 125,000 books and has subscriptions to 1,700 magazines and journals, as well as CD-ROMs and commercial database services. The library's collection is divided into three sections—Reference, Circulating, and Historical Intelligence. Besides traditional reference tools like encyclopedias, atlases and dictionaries, the CIA Library contains diplomatic lists and foreign and domestic phone books.

Although the CIA and its surroundings offer a fascinating glimpse into the sense of history that encompasses the agency's employees, the headquarters is still a modern office in which intelligence is gathered, analyzed, and distributed. There is a clear organization that shapes each of these functions.

6

The Path of Intelligence

The CIA's primary mission, as noted on its Web site, is to serve as "the eyes and ears of the nation and at times its hidden hand." According to the CIA, this is to be accomplished by: collecting intelligence that matters; providing relevant, timely, and objective all-source analysis; and conducting covert action at the direction of the president to pre-empt threats or achieve U.S. policy objectives.

The basis of all of this—the key to accomplishing these goals—lies in intelligence. But what exactly is intelligence? And how does this intelligence help the CIA carry out its mission?

Intelligence is essentially information—information that is gathered from a variety of sources. The information may be provided by human sources—either spies or informants. This information may be gathered using technology— satellites, wiretaps, Web sites, or e-mail postings, for example. Once the information has been gathered, it is analyzed. If it is in code, it must be decrypted. Then it is compared with other information to form a more complete picture of a situation, a person, or a potential threat. At this stage, the information can properly be described as "intelligence."

The CIA is in the business of gathering and analyzing intelligence. This intelligence gives CIA analysts—and ultimately U.S. policymakers—information about what is taking place around the world, information that will help them understand global events and make predictions about ways to respond to these events and what their outcomes might be. CIA analysts do not make policy decisions or otherwise determine how the intelligence will be used to affect U.S. foreign policy—that is the job of the president, the State Department, the Defense Department, and Congress. The CIA provides the intelligence, which those policymakers use to make decisions about American foreign policy or security.

The CIA needs to provide policymakers with timely, relevant information that focuses on: current developments around the world; reports (biographies and studies) of the key players in these events; warnings of possible crises or threats to the United States; technical analyses of weapons and weapon systems; reports on specific topics, countries, or foreign policy issues; and reports on topics that might have been requested by the policymakers. The CIA's role is critical because it can provide information not easily available from sources like newspapers or diplomats working in a particular region. Often the CIA obtains information from sources whose identities must be kept confidential. For this reason, much of the intelligence produced by the CIA is classified—it is not available to the general public, only to those who can be trusted to keep its contents secret.

THE INTELLIGENCE CYCLE

The first step in the intelligence cycle is the collection or gathering of the information that will become intelligence. Two divisions within the CIA are responsible for gathering information—the National Clandestine Service (NCS), which was formerly the Directorate of Operations, and the Directorate of Science and Technology (DS&T). The NCS is responsible for information collected by clandestine, or secret, means, including human sources. It is also responsible for the overt collection of foreign intelligence provided by people and organizations within the United States. The DS&T uses technology to gather information or to respond to intelligence needs. The DS&T also researches, designs, and deploys specialized intelligence systems.

Once the information has been gathered, it must be analyzed and then checked and combined with other existing information and data to produce intelligence on specific issues. This is the responsibility of the Directorate of Intelligence (DI), which analyzes intelligence from all of the different sources and produces briefings, reports, and papers. The DI is responsible for ensuring not only the accuracy of the intelligence but also its timeliness and relevance.

The CIA's Directorate of Science and Technology celebrated its fortieth anniversary in 2003 by revealing a few of its secrets at the CIA Museum at the agency's headquarters. On display was the robot catfish "Charlie," built in 2000. It is a realistic swimming robot, though the agency would not disclose much more about its mission.

Policymakers and those for whom the CIA provides intelligence are often referred to as "consumers." These consumers include the White House, the Department of State, Congress, the Department of Defense, the FBI, and various other governmental agencies.

Five types of intelligence can be provided to consumers: current intelligence, which deals with day-to-day events and may include details of new events and their possible significance; estimative intelligence, which

DIFFERENT KINDS OF INTELLIGENCE

COMINT: Communications Intelligence comes from intercepted foreign communications.

ELINT: Electronic Intelligence is technical and intelligence information taken from intercepted foreign electromagnetic transmissions.

HUMINT: Human Intelligence is information gathered by human sources through covert and other methods.

IMINT: Imagery Intelligence comes from satellite photography or other imagery that is then analyzed and processed.

MASINT: Measurement and Signature Intelligence is technically derived intelligence taken from nuclear, optical, radio-frequency, acoustics, seismic, and materials sciences data.

OPEN SOURCE: Open source information is public and available to everyone, such as information from newspapers and magazines, news broadcasts, and the Internet.

SIGINT: Signals Intelligence is information that comes from intercepted signals, and includes COMINT, ELINT, and MASINT.

discusses predictions or possible events rather than events that have taken place and is designed to fill in the gaps between known facts; warning intelligence, which identifies events that might impact U.S. foreign policy or require a military response; research intelligence, generally a more in-depth study on a particular topic, country, or individual; and scientific intelligence, which is information on the development of foreign technologies and weapons systems.

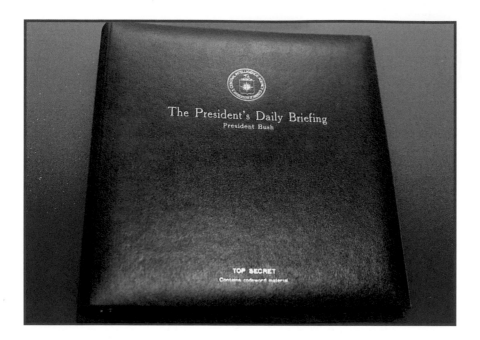

The President's Daily Briefing binder was on display in 2002 in the *Spies: Secrets From the CIA, KGB, and Hollywood* exhibit at the Ronald Reagan Presidential Library Foundation in Simi Valley, California. The binder was on loan from the White House for the exhibit. The President's Daily Briefing, also known as the President's Daily Brief, contains intelligence about key security concerns.

The DI is perhaps best known for two publications—the President's Daily Briefing and the Senior Executive Intelligence Brief. The President's Daily Briefing contains intelligence about key security concerns and issues of interest to the president. The brief is distributed only to the president, the vice president, and a small group of Cabinet-level officials approved by the president. The Senior Executive Intelligence Brief, which is also distributed daily, provides critical intelligence to senior policy and security officials and is coordinated with other intelligence agencies. Intelligence from this brief is often sent to U.S. military commands. Because both briefs are highly classified, they are distributed only to a very select group of people.

Besides the DI, the NCS, and the DS&T, the CIA has a fourth directorate—the Directorate of Support (DS). This division is responsible for areas like CIA personnel, training, human resources, maintenance of the facilities, medical services, records management, and declassification.

Although much of the intelligence produced by the CIA is classified, certain resources produced by the DI are available to the general public. These include the World Factbook, an annual reference guide that lists information on the countries of the world, and the Chiefs of State and Cabinet Members of Foreign Governments directory, which is updated weekly and provides a listing of the principal policymakers in countries around the world. Both of these can be found on the CIA Web site.

HOW INFORMATION BECOMES CLASSIFIED

Much of the intelligence produced by the CIA contains information that is secret. It may concern details that will impact U.S. security. It may contain information about world leaders or about events that will destabilize another country. It may contain data about weapons systems or critical technology. It may have been provided by individuals whose identities must be kept secret.

For this reason, many CIA reports are distributed only to a small, very select group of people. Similarly, the information is classified to indicate who is able to access that information and under what circumstances.

The system used by the CIA is the same system used by the rest of the federal government. This system divides, or "classifies," information into three categories: confidential, secret, and top secret.

Confidential information is information related to national security that must be protected. If it is distributed without permission, it could impact the security of the United States.

Secret information is national security information that must be substantially protected. The unauthorized release of this information could cause serious damage to U.S. security.

Top-secret information is national security information that requires the highest degree of protection. If disclosed without permission, top-secret information can be expected to cause very severe damage to national security.

Many laws and regulations govern classified information. Because of these laws, certain intelligence automatically becomes declassified and is available after a specified period of time. Very sensitive information is protected from these laws and remains classified.

THE INTELLIGENCE COMMUNITY

After the September 11, 2001, attacks on the United States, congressional and independent task forces investigated possible weaknesses in the system of intelligence-sharing that might have contributed to a lack of preparation or anticipation of the terrorist actions. President George W.

Bush ultimately authorized sweeping changes in the structure of the intelligence community; these changes directly impacted the CIA.

First and foremost, President Bush separated the offices of director of intelligence and director of the CIA, creating two separate positions. The first director of national intelligence, John Negroponte, was sworn into office in April 2005. He served in the position until January 2007. The director of the CIA now reports to the director of national intelligence.

The changes were also designed to ensure greater sharing of intelligence among certain government agencies. These agencies now form part of what is called the "intelligence community." Besides the CIA, these agencies include the intelligence divisions of the armed forces (Army, Air Force, Coast Guard, Marine Corps, and Navy), the Defense Intelligence Agency, the Department of Homeland Security, the Department of Energy, the Department of State, the Department of the Treasury, the Drug Enforcement Administration, the FBI, the National Security Agency, the National Geospatial-Intelligence Agency, and the National Reconnaissance Office. The goal is to establish effective links so that all of the intelligence gathered by these separate agencies can be used to give a more complete picture of events critical to America's security.

WHO MANAGES THE CIA?

The director of the CIA now reports to the director of national intelligence, who oversees the intelligence activities of all members of the intelligence community. The

President George W. Bush stood by during the ceremonial swearing-in of John Negroponte in 2005 as the first director of national intelligence. The position was created in response to the terrorist attacks of September 11, 2001. The director of the CIA now reports to the director of national intelligence.

responsibilities of the director of the CIA reflect the overall goals of the CIA. These include the collection of intelligence (from human and other sources); the analysis of this intelligence based on its relationship to national security and the distribution of relevant intelligence; the assurance that the best use is made of resources and that the risks to the people who collect intelligence are minimized; and any other duties related to intelligence that affect U.S. security as directed by the president and the director of national intelligence.

Other senior positions within the CIA include the deputy director of the CIA, who assists the director and performs his duties when he is absent, and the associate deputy director of the CIA, who manages the CIA on a day-to-day basis. Each separate division of the CIA—the Directorate of Intelligence, the National Clandestine Service, the Directorate of Science and Technology, and the Directorate of Support—has a director who is responsible for day-to-day management.

There is also a director for the CIA's Center for the Study of Intelligence, which maintains the CIA's historical materials.

The Office of General Counsel, which provides legal counsel for the CIA and advises its director on all legal matters, also has a principal director, known as the general counsel. Finally, the Office of Public Affairs, which is the communications tool for the CIA and provides media, public policy, and employee communications, has its own director.

Throughout the CIA, staff members may be engaged in clandestine or undercover work and need to keep their identities secret. This is also true of senior CIA staff members; not all of the directors of the different divisions are publicly named, as some may be working undercover, connected to colleagues working undercover, or otherwise engaged in missions that may require that their identities be kept secret.

7

WORKING FOR
THE CIA

Because work at the CIA involves so many different
fields, skills, and locations, there is no such thing as a
"typical" CIA employee. When we think of a person who
works for the CIA, we most often think of a spy—someone
working undercover in a foreign country, providing critical
bits of information to help protect the United States.

There are, of course, these kinds of positions within the
CIA. People whom we might call "spies" work for the CIA's
National Clandestine Service (NCS). They are called intelligence officers. They work undercover in foreign countries to collect intelligence. Often they do this by recruiting
other people—foreign agents—to work with them and
supply them with information. They might recruit agents

The U.S. Senate Select Intelligence Committee and the U.S. House Select Intelligence Committee heard testimony from a CIA officer and a New York FBI agent during a joint hearing in September 2002. The hearing was held to examine intelligence failures before the 9/11 terrorist attacks. The identities of the two speakers are protected by a screen. CIA intelligence officers, or "spies," keep their identities hidden. Sometimes, friends or even family members do not know they work for the CIA.

who work in government offices, in secure facilities, or in other locations where they would be positioned to obtain information about people or policies. The intelligence officers keep their identities hidden; even close friends and family might not realize that they are employed by the CIA. Often, they also work at a "day" job as part of their cover. There is, of course, a certain amount of danger involved in their work. Depending on their assignment, they may need to blend into a foreign culture, assume a false identity, or adopt different customs and habits.

The skills that make a good intelligence officer include an appreciation for travel and for other cultures. Proficiency in foreign languages is vital, as is a strong educational background. Perhaps most important is a willingness to accept anonymity—to understand that when you success-fully perform your job, only a very small group of people will ever know what you have done or appreciate the sac-rifices involved.

Not everyone who works for the National Clandes-tine Service is a spy. The collection management officers guide intelligence collection, serving as a link between the intelligence officers and the government officials who determine foreign policy. The collection management of-ficers must determine what policymakers and intelligence analysts need to know and relay that information to the intelligence officers. Also vital to the work of the Clandes-tine Service are the staff operations officers, who mainly work at the CIA headquarters near Washington. These officers provide research and support to their colleagues who are stationed overseas. This work includes monitor-ing counterintelligence issues and providing help in deal-ing with foreign contacts.

Perhaps understandably, the people who work for the Directorate of Science and Technology are, in general, people who love problem-solving using science, engineer-ing, and other forms of technology. DS&T personnel use technology to gather different forms of intelligence; they also must design and develop new systems to protect the security of these intelligence-gathering methods.

Employees of the NCS and the DS&T are the people who gather the information; analysis and distribution of this information in the form of intelligence briefings and reports are handled by the Directorate of Intelligence. A successful DI employee enjoys the kind of work required to review different pieces of information and form them into a cohesive, comprehensive picture. This requires skills in research, in writing, and in analyzing information. DI employees often work under tight deadlines. Besides writing skills, DI staff may be called upon to deliver briefings or reports before small or large groups of people, so they must also have the skills necessary to speak before an audience.

The CIA also needs the services of a wide range of support staff to ensure that each directorate operates smoothly. People with skills in foreign languages are needed, as are people with expertise in auditing and finance. Other support staff members are skilled in law or medicine, information technology, geography, graphic design, teaching, and administrative work.

There is no single program of study a student should pursue if he or she is interested in a career with the CIA. It is helpful to know a foreign language, especially one of the following: Arabic, Chinese, Farsi, Japanese, Korean, Russian, Serbo-Croatian, or Turkish. All CIA employees must be U.S. citizens. Most have a college degree; many have graduate degrees as well. Applicants must undergo a background check, a polygraph examination, and a medical examination as part of the application process.

In September 2006, *Business Week* magazine named the CIA as one of the top 50 employers for new college graduates. The agency was ranked thirty-second, amid such private-sector corporations as the Walt Disney Co., General Electric, and Southwest Airlines, and other government agencies like the U.S. State Department and the Internal Revenue Service. The rankings were based on information from college career centers, undergraduates, and the companies and agencies.

The exact number of people who work for the CIA is classified. The budget of the CIA is also not released.

BEHIND THE SCENES

As we have learned, not all of those who work at the CIA are directly involved in intelligence work. In fact, not all of those who work for the CIA are human!

The CIA employs a K-9 Corps, a team of elite dogs trained to guard CIA employees. The K-9 Corps was formed in 1991, at the time that the United States was involved in the Persian Gulf War. The dogs were trained to protect the agency from a terrorist attack.

Since an important part of the K-9 Corps' work involves finding explosives, the dogs go through a 13-week course in explosives-detection training. The dogs' sensitive noses

Staff members work in the CIA Headquarters in Langley, Virginia. Although there is no single program of study that students interested in CIA careers should pursue, proficiency in a foreign language is one skill that the CIA encourages.

are able to detect many scents that humans cannot. As part of their training, the K-9 Corps dogs are exposed to as many as 19,000 explosives scents that they must learn to detect. A final exam is even held at the end of the 13-week course—dogs and their human partners are tested on 10 explosives searches (conducted indoors and outdoors).

Certain members of the K-9 Corps also undergo 13 weeks of street training, during which they learn skills that require speed and accuracy. At the end of the street training, the dogs undergo a final exam in agility, obedience training, article search, suspect search, and criminal apprehension (catching criminals).

The K-9 Corps do not work exclusively at CIA Headquarters. Some work with other law enforcement teams, like police departments or the Drug Enforcement Administration. They may also be sent to major events like the Super Bowl or other places where large crowds might gather.

WHY IT MATTERS

The mission of the CIA is to collect, evaluate, and provide foreign intelligence to the president and senior government policymakers to help them make decisions about national security. But what does this mean for ordinary Americans? How does the work of the CIA impact us?

First, it is important to know that the CIA is not spying on you or keeping records of your activities. The CIA is prohibited by law from gathering intelligence on U.S. citizens on U.S. soil. The CIA's focus is on gathering information related to foreign intelligence and foreign counterintelligence. The CIA can only gather intelligence on U.S. citizens when there is a specific intelligence reason for doing so—for example, if there is evidence that a certain individual may be involved in international terrorist activities or espionage. This type of intelligence gathering would require approval from senior CIA staff members, the director of national intelligence, or the U.S. attorney general.

The CIA deals exclusively with the collection, analysis, and distribution of foreign intelligence. It is not involved in law enforcement and does not have the power to arrest or detain suspects.

Covert actions undertaken by the CIA require the approval of the president and are normally recommended by the president's National Security Council. These actions are generally recommended when the National Security Council believes that diplomacy will not achieve a particular foreign policy goal and when military intervention would be too drastic an option. Often the role of the U.S. government in these actions will not be admitted or known by the public. The intelligence oversight committees of Congress are notified when these actions are undertaken.

Because much of the work of the CIA is classified, the typical American may not be aware of how CIA efforts are contributing to the protection of U.S. interests. But CIA analysts play a critical role in the war against terrorism by collecting and analyzing information on foreign terrorist groups and individuals. CIA analysts provide detailed reports on global events to help the president and his policymakers respond. They provide background information on world leaders to help senior government officials better understand the men and women with whom they are dealing. CIA analysts predict changes in governments or pending conflicts, information that can be used to protect Americans living and working in those regions of the world.

THE CENTRAL INTELLIGENCE AGENCY

The CIA was created to do, in peacetime, what the OSS had done during wartime—protect American security. The key to this protection was intelligence. Since 1947, the CIA has focused on collecting and analyzing this intelligence so that the president and senior policymakers can respond to a changing world, to new threats and new situations.

Much of what the CIA does is invisible to most Americans. When the CIA performs a mission successfully—warning of a possible threat, providing information about an event that will impact the United States so that government

DECLASSIFIED INFORMATION

★ ★ ★ ★ ★

After a certain specified period of time, reports, briefings, and other intelligence communications created by the CIA are declassified and become available to the public. A search through this data, available through the Freedom of Information Act, provides fascinating insight into the scope of the CIA's investigations, ranging from reports of unidentified flying objects to detailed studies of global events and information about the status of prisoners of war and soldiers whose remains have never been recovered. The following Senior Executive Intelligence Brief, now declassified, is from August 1999:

Sudan: Denying Chemical Weapons Investigation

Khartoum has backtracked from earlier statements welcoming a UN investigation into allegations of chemical weapons (CW) use in southern Sudan and is demanding a quid pro quo US agreement to officials can respond promptly—we may never hear about it. It is only on the occasions when a failure has occurred— when a terrorist eludes capture or when an attack or event is not anticipated—that the CIA is put in the spotlight and questions are asked about the work that is done at Langley and around the world.

In a speech made in July 1995, President William Clinton noted the value of the information he received from the CIA: "Every morning I start my day with an intelligence report. The intelligence I receive informs just about every foreign policy decision we make. It's easy to take it

a UN investigation of the strike on the al-Shifa pharmaceutical plant in Khartoum, according to Sudanese media reports. Sudan—which in May ratified the Chemical Weapons Convention—denies that it has produced or used CW against southern rebels.

—*An investigation of the al-Shifa facility would be unlikely to yield conclusive CW evidence because of the time that has elapsed since the strike.*

The UN and relief organizations are increasingly concerned about reports from relief workers that chemical bombs were used against two rebel villages late last month. *The reports, however, are contradictory and probably exaggerated to serve the rebels' political agenda.*

—*An assessment of reported symptoms does not suggest the use of traditional lethal CW agents, but samples being analyzed by international organizations may yield more information on the agents used.*

for granted, but we couldn't do without it. Unique intelligence makes it less likely that our forces will be sent into battle, less likely that American lives will have to be put at risk. It gives us a chance to prevent crises instead of forcing us to manage them."

President George H.W. Bush, who had served as director of central intelligence, emphasized the importance he placed on the agency's work in a speech at the swearing-in of Robert Gates as director of central intelligence in November 1991: "Intelligence remains our basic national instrument for anticipating dangers—military, political, and economic. Intelligence is and always will be our first line of defense, enabling us to ward off emerging threats whenever possible before any damage is done. It can also be a means of anticipating opportunities."

GLOSSARY

cabinet A body of official advisors to a president; in the United States, it consists of the heads of various government departments.

capitalism An economic system in which all or most of the means of production and distribution—such as land, factories, communications, and transportation— are privately owned and operated in a relatively competitive environment.

classified Secret or confidential and available only to authorized people.

Cold War The ideological conflict between the United States and the Soviet Union during the last half of the twentieth century; the conflict never led to direct military action.

communism Any economic theory or system based on the ownership of all property by the community as a whole.

counterespionage Actions to prevent or thwart espionage by the enemy.

counterintelligence Organized activity of an intelligence service designed to block an enemy's sources of information, to deceive the enemy, to prevent sabotage, and to gather political and military information.

covert Not openly shown, engaged in, or acknowledged.

decrypt To decode.

defector A person who forsakes one cause, party, or nation for another, often because of a change in ideology.

diplomacy The art and practice of conducting relations between nations.

double agent A spy who pretends to serve one government while actually serving another.

espionage The use of spies to obtain information about the plans and activities of a foreign government or a competing company.

intelligence Information concerning an enemy or a potential enemy; the evaluated conclusions or analysis drawn from such information.

Joint Chiefs of Staff A group within the Department of Defense consisting of the chief of staff of the Army, the chief of naval operations, the chief of staff of the Air Force, the commandant of the Marine Corps, a director, and a chairman.

paramilitary Forces that work along with, or in place of, a regular military organization, often as a semi-official or secret auxiliary.

propaganda Any systematic effort to spread or promote particular ideas or beliefs to further a cause or to damage an opposing one.

sabotage Destructive or obstructive action taken by a civilian or an enemy agent to hinder a nation's war effort.

spy A person employed by a government to get secret information about or monitor another government.

superpower Any of the few top world powers competing with one another for international influence.

wiretap A concealed listening device used on telephone or telegraph wires to obtain information.

BIBLIOGRAPHY

Breckinridge, Scott D. *The CIA and the U.S. Intelligence System*. Boulder, Colo.: Westview Press, 1986.

Brown, Anthony Cave. *The Last Hero: Wild Bill Donovan*. New York: Times Books, 1982.

Center for the Study of Intelligence, *"Our First Line of Defense": Presidential Reflections on U.S. Intelligence*. Washington, D.C.: Center for the Study of Intelligence, 1996.

Central Intelligence Agency, *A Consumer's Guide to Intelligence*. Washington, D.C.: Central Intelligence Agency, 1999.

Ellis, Joseph J. *His Excellency: George Washington*. New York: Alfred A. Knopf, 2004.

Ford, Corey. *Donovan of OSS*. Boston: Little, Brown & Co., 1970.

Jeffreys-Jones, Rhodri. *The CIA and American Democracy*. New Haven, Conn.: Yale University Press, 1989.

Ranelagh, John. *The Agency: The Rise and Decline of the CIA*. New York: Simon and Schuster, 1986.

Richelson, Jeffrey T. *The Wizards of Langley: Inside the CIA's Directorate of Science and Technology*. Boulder, Colo.: Westview Press, 2001.

Smith, R. Harris. *OSS: The Secret History of America's First Central Intelligence Agency*. Berkeley, Calif.: University of California Press, 1972.

Steury, Donald P. (ed.). *On the Front Lines of the Cold War:*

Documents on the Intelligence War in Berlin, 1946 to 1961.
Washington, D.C.: Center for the Study of Intelligence,
1999.

Web sites

Central Intelligence Agency
www.cia.gov

Central Intelligence Agency: Electronic Reading Room
www.foia.cia.gov

United States Intelligence Community
www.intelligence.gov

The New York Times
www.nytimes.com

The Washington Post
www.washingtonpost.com

FURTHER READING

Allen, Thomas B. *George Washington, Spymaster: How the Americans Outspied the British and Won the Revolutionary War*. New York: National Geographic Children's Books, 2004.

Brown, Anthony Cave. *The Last Hero: Wild Bill Donovan*. New York: Times Books, 1982.

Fleming, Fergus. *Tales of Real Spies*. Tulsa, Okla.: E.D.C. Publishing, 1998.

Koestler-Grack, Rachel A. *Nathan Hale: Courageous Spy*. Philadelphia: Chelsea House Publishers, 2005.

Kronenwetter, Michael. *Covert Action*. Danbury, Conn.: Franklin Watts, 1991.

O'Donnell, Patrick K. *Operatives, Spies, and Saboteurs: The Unknown Story of the Men and Women of World War II's OSS*. New York: Free Press, 2004.

O'Toole, G.J.A. *Honorable Treachery: A History of U.S. Intelligence, Espionage, and Covert Action From the American Revolution to the CIA*. New York: Atlantic Monthly Press, 1993.

Web sites

America's CryptoKids: Future Codemakers and Codebreakers
www.nsa.gov/kids/

America's Story From America's Library
www.americasstory.gov

CIA's Homepage for Kids
https://www.cia.gov/cia/ciakids/index.shtml

Defense Intelligence Agency for Kids
www.dia.mil/kids/interfacemx.html

National Geospatial-Intelligence Agency Children's Site
www.nga.mil/ngakids/

National Reconnaissance Organization's NROjr
www.nrojr.gov

Nova: Spies That Fly
www.pbs.org/wgbh/nova/spiesfly/

Nova: Submarines, Secrets, and Spies
www.pbs.org/wgbh/nova/subsecrets/

The World Factbook
https://www.cia.gov/cia/publications/factbook/index.html

PICTURE CREDITS

INDEX

ABOUT THE AUTHOR

Heather Lehr Wagner is a writer and an editor. She is the author of more than 30 books exploring social and political issues and focusing on the lives of prominent men and women. She earned a B.A. in political science from Duke University and an M.A. in government from the College of William and Mary. She lives with her husband and family in Pennsylvania.